Communities Today and Tomorrow

Polly Goodman

Gareth Stevens
Publishing

Please visit our website, www.garethstevens.com.
For a free color catalogue of all our high-quality books,
call toll free 1-800-542-2595 or fax 1-877-542-2596.

Library of Congress Cataloging-in-Publication Data

Goodman, Polly.
Communities today and tomorrow / Polly Goodman.
    p. cm. — (Earth alert!)
Includes index.
ISBN 978-1-4339-5999-8 (library binding)
1. Communities—Juvenile literature. I. Title.
HM756.G66 2011
307—dc22

2010049257

This edition first published in 2012 by
Gareth Stevens Publishing
111 East 14th Street, Suite 349
New York, NY 10003

Copyright © 2012 Wayland/Gareth Stevens Publishing

Editorial Director: Kerri O'Donnell
Design Director: Haley Harasymiw

Printed in China

CPSIA compliance information. Batch WAS11GS. For further information contact Gareth Stevens, New York, New York at 1-800-542-2595

Picture acknowledgements
Cover: Shutterstock; Alphen aan den Rijn Information 29; Axiom
Photographic Agency 17 (Jim Holmes); James Davis Travel Photography 7; Eye Ubiqui tous 18 (Paul Hutley), 21 and 24
(Paul Thompson); Getty Images 1 (Jerry Alexander), 4 (Michel Setboun), 5 (Oliver Benn), 10 (Nicholas DeVore), 11
(Sue Cunningham), 16 (J eremy Walker), 20 (Johan Elzenga), 25 (Robert A Mitchell), 27 (David Hanover); Hodder
Wayland Picture Library 3 (Julia Waterlow), 14, 19 Impact Photos 8 (Mark Henley), 9 (Mark Henley), 12 (Alan
Keohane),13 (Mark Henley), 15 (Sergio Dorantes), 22 (David Silverberg), 23 (Philip Gordon), 28 (Mark Henley); Alex
Robb 6 (both); Stephanie Turner 26 (both). Dustbin information on page 19 courtesy of Ecoschools, Tidy Britain Group.
Artwork by Peter Bull Art Studio.

Contents

What Are Settlements?

Settlements are places where groups of people live. They can be tiny hamlets or villages in the countryside, with only a few houses. Or they can be large towns and cities, with thousands of people.

Settlements in the countryside are called rural settlements. Towns and cities are urban settlements.

These homes in Mongolia belong to nomads, people who move from place to place with their animals. ()

All settlements need to be able to get water, food, and fuel for cooking. They also need materials to build homes. These are people's basic needs.

The History of Settlements

People started to live in settlements about 12,000 years ago. Before this, they wandered from place to place, hunting animals and gathering plants for food.

Villages and towns grew up near fertile land, where farmers could grow food. Many began beside rivers, which provided water and travel routes. Much later, settlements grew up beside roads and railroads.

Some towns grew for special reasons. Ports developed on rivers and coasts where boats came to shore. Industrial towns with factories became manufacturing centers.

⋂ **The walls of this town in Spain protected its people.**

TYPES OF SETTLEMENT

TYPE	NUMBER OF PEOPLE
Hamlet	Fewer than 50
Village	50 to 1,000
Town	1,000 to 100,000
City	Over 100,000

A VILLAGE IN INDONESIA

Kenari is a village on the island of Flores, in Indonesia. Most people are farmers. They grow rice in fields nearby. There is a school, a post office, and one small shop in the village.

The houses in Kenari have been built using bamboo and rattan, which are local plants. Since there is no electricity, people cook on fires, burning wood they have gathered nearby. They use oil lamps for light.

There are no roads to Kenari. People have to walk to the nearest market, which is 8 miles (13 km) away.

Houses in Kenari are built on stilts to keep them cool. ↻

Children in Kenari after school. ⊃

The Growth of Cities

Since the 1700s, cities have grown rapidly as centers of manufacturing and business. In the twentieth century, cities grew even faster. Cities have grown because the population of the world has been rising. But they have also grown because more and more people have been moving to cities from the countryside.

Cities attract people because there are more jobs to do than in the countryside. There are more schools, hospitals, and forms of entertainment.

◐ The center of New York City is an island called Manhattan.

A tiny apartment in Tokyo, Japan, the biggest city in the world. ➲

Cities Today

Cities are still growing today and they are constantly changing. Every day, workers build new offices and homes. There is so little space that modern buildings are usually tall, so they take up less room on the ground.

In the center of overcrowded cities, many people live in very small homes. Outside city centers, suburbs are growing and the edges of cities are creeping outward.

THE TEN LARGEST CITIES IN 2010

	Millions of people
1. Tokyo, Japan	36.7
2. Delhi, India	22.2
3. São Paulo, Brazil	20.3
4. Mumbai, India	20.0
5. Mexico City, Mexico	19.5
6. New York City, U.S.A.	19.4
7. Shanghai, China	16.6
8. Calcutta, India	15.6
9. Dhaka, Bangladesh	14.6
10. Karachi, Pakistan	13.1

Activity

HISTORY DETECTIVE

Do you live in a village, town, or city? What do you think it was like 100 years ago?
Go to your local library and find the oldest map of where you live. Then compare it with a modern map. What is similar and what is different? Why do you think the settlement grew where it is?

New, tall office buildings and older houses in the city of Shanghai, China. ↻

Cities and the Environment

Cities use up huge amounts of energy and produce tons of waste every year. Many cities are very polluted. Pollution from traffic and factories that hangs in the air can damage people's health. City waste can pour into rivers and pollute the water, and many cities are running out of places to put their garbage.

Homes and Buildings

Shelter is another basic need. Everyone needs protection from the rain, the sun, and the cold.

Thousands of years ago, the first homes were huts made from materials found nearby. Trees were cut down for wood. Clay, earth, and stone were dug up from the ground. Many people, especially in poorer countries, still live in homes made just from local materials.

These houses in Lesotho, Africa, are made of stone, earth, and wood. ↻

SHANTYTOWNS

In poor countries around the world, many people move to the cities looking for work. The new arrivals are usually poor and cannot afford to pay for housing. So they build shelters from cheap material they find, including sheets of metal, scraps of wood, and pieces of plastic.

These settlements are called shantytowns. They are normally on the edges of big cities, built on land that no one else wants.

⋂ A shantytown on the outskirts of Rio de Janeiro, in Brazil.

Modern Buildings

Modern buildings include many materials that are made in factories, such as brick, cement, metal, glass, and plastic. They are often carried long distances on trucks, trains, and ships.

As the population increases and people need more homes, we are taking vast quantities of building materials from the environment. Whole forests are cut down, and stone is dug from huge quarries.

Energy

We use energy all the time. We use huge amounts for heating, lighting, cooking, transportation, and to run machines.

Energy comes from many different sources. It can come from burning wood, coal, gas, or oil. It can also come from the wind, the sun, and moving water.

These African women have gathered wood to use for cooking. Wood is their only source of energy. ↻

More energy is used in towns and cities than in smaller settlements. There are more homes, offices, streets, and factories, which all need power. Machines such as computers, televisions, and refrigerators use up electricity. Cars and trucks burn gas and oil.

Global Warming

Coal, oil, and gas are taken from the earth. If we continue using so much energy, these fuels may run out.

When coal, oil, and gas are burned, they release smoke and gases. This air pollution makes it difficult for some people to breathe. The smoke and gases also rise up into the earth's atmosphere. These "greenhouse gases" act like a blanket, keeping the earth warm.

Most scientists agree that we are burning so much fuel that we are making the earth too warm. The polar ice caps are likely to melt. Sea levels will rise due to the melting ice and the warmer ocean water, which expands as it heats up. Low-lying areas will be flooded.

⋒ Cars, buses, and trucks cause traffic jams and air pollution in towns and cities.

Food

People in towns and cities rely on farmers in the countryside to grow their food. Wealthy countries import foods from all around the world so that people have a wide variety to choose from.

Tons of food has to be transported into settlements every day using trucks, trains, ships, and airplanes. Many trucks and ships use refrigerators to keep food cool. All this transportation uses up more fuel and causes air pollution (see page 13). Roads become blocked with traffic jams in the cities and the countryside.

⊂ Oranges are grown in hot countries and may be transported hundreds of thousands of miles to supermarkets in other lands.

Supermarkets

In many wealthy countries, most people buy their food from large supermarkets. Since there is little space in town and city centers, new supermarkets are usually built on the outskirts. They have parking lots so people can drive to them from all over the area.

⋂ An "out of town" shopping center in Mexico.

Activity

FOOD MAP

Most foods from supermarkets have labels telling you the state or country of origin.

1. Collect food labels from different types of food.
2. Trace a U.S. map and a world map from an atlas.
3. Look at the labels, find the state or country where each food came from, and label them on the maps.
4. Draw lines from each place to your hometown.

Water

People in towns and cities use huge amounts of water every day. In wealthy countries, water is piped to people's homes from reservoirs (lakes for storin water) or from undergrou

Before the water reaches our faucets, it passes throu treatment works to make i safe to drink. Most used water passes through sewa works before being returne to rivers or the sea.

WATER USE

Water used in everyday activities:

Washing hands and face	2.5 gallons (9 L)
Brushing teeth (faucet off)	0.25 gallons (1 L)
Flushing a toilet	1.5 gallons (6 L)
Taking a shower	8 gallons (30 L)
Taking a bath	24 gallons (90 L)
Running washing machine	32 gallons (120 L)
Drinking/cooking per person	1.5 gallons (6 L)
Dishwasher	13 gallons (50 L)

Sometimes dirty water runs straight into rivers and the sea, polluting the water and killing wildlife. ➲

Not Enough Water

Rain does not fall equally around the world. People in many countries do not have enough water. Without faucets in their homes, many people have to travel long distances to find and carry water.

All water in the world is part of a cycle, called the water cycle. The water we use is replaced by rain. But if we use too much water, it cannot be replaced fast enough. Water levels in rivers and underground are falling because we are using too much water.

∩ Carrying water in Bangladesh.

Activity

1. Add up the amount of water you use every day, using the table on page 16.

2. If you used a bucket that held 2.5 gallons (9 L), how many buckets would you need to fill and carry every day if you didn't have faucets in your home?

Waste and Recycling

People in towns and cities produce tons of waste every day, which all has to be taken away.

In many countries, sewage and dirty water pass through sewage works. But sometimes, especially in poorer countries, dirty water runs straight into rivers and the sea, and can cause disease.

Solid waste such as packaging is burned or buried underground. Plastic and other waste stays underground forever and fills up the ground. Many cities are running out of places to bury their garbage. Garbage dumps can pollute the air and water, and cause disease.

A bulldozer burying garbage in a dump, called a landfill site. ⊃

Recycling

Recycling changes some types of garbage into material that can be used again. It can help reduce the waste that we bury underground.

Paper, glass, plastic, aluminum, and tin cans can all be recycled. To recycle, we have to separate the material that can be recycled from the rest of our garbage.

Textiles 2%

Metals 7%

Glass 8%

Plastics 8%

Food and Garden Waste 30%

Paper and Board 33%

Other 12%

A TYPICAL TRASH CAN

This is the content of an average trash can from a house in a wealthy country.

⋂ Garbage is separated into a recycling truck.

TRUE STORY

FORT LAUDERDALE, FLORIDA

In Fort Lauderdale, every home has two special containers for garbage that can be recycled. One is for paper and card. The other is for glass bottles, drink cartons, plastic bottles, and cans. Every week, the containers are emptied.

At the beach, there are bright blue recycling containers for bottles and cans.

The city also has "GreenWorks" volunteers, who encourage people to recycle as much as possible.

City Zones

Large cities often have different areas, or zones, each with a special function. Most people work in a commercial zone, where there are stores, banks, and offices. Areas of factories and workshops are called industrial zones.

The places where most of the buildings are homes are called residential areas. The oldest residential areas are close to the city center, in the inner city.

The chimneys of an industrial zone behind a residential area. ⟲

Traveling Across the City

Thousands of people travel to work in cities every day. Many travel from one side of a city to another. Others travel in from the countryside, or towns outside the city.

Cars, buses, trains, and bicycles carry people to work. Roads often become blocked by traffic jams, especially in the rush hours, and the air can be filled with unpleasant traffic fumes.

People who walk, cycle, or use public transportation, such as trains and buses, help to cut the amount of air pollution and congestion in cities. They reduce the number of vehicles needed to carry people around.

⌒ Office workers in the morning rush hour in London, in the UK.

Entertainment and Leisure

Every city has many different ways for people to spend their spare time. Indoors there are movie theaters, museums, bars, and restaurants.

Outside areas include parks, playgrounds, sports fields, and swimming pools. Parks are also habitats for plants and animals.

Central Park, in the middle of New York City. ○

Planning Growth

Many cities around the world are growing too fast. But others are controlled by planners, who usually work for the government. Planners decide whether new buildings should be built, and where they will be.

There are different ideas about planning cities. Some people think residential areas should be kept separate from commercial zones, to make residential areas more attractive places to live. Others believe people should live close to their work, so they travel less and there is less traffic.

Changing Cities

Cities all over the world are getting bigger, because populations grow and more people move to cities from the countryside. Today, about 50 percent of the world's population live in cities. By 2030, this figure is expected to grow to 60 percent.

⋒ **High-rise apartment buildings in Hong Kong.**

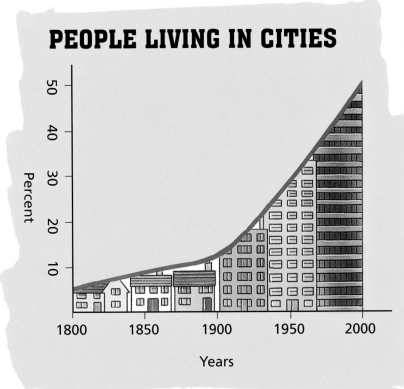

PEOPLE LIVING IN CITIES

Percent

50 40 30 20 10

1800   1850   1900   1950   2000

Years

In city centers, where there is very little space, new apartment buildings are often built with many stories. They can fit more homes for people on a small area of land than lower buildings provide.

Out of Town

Since the early 1980s, many businesses have moved out of crowded city centers to business parks on the city outskirts. Business parks have space for parking lots, so most people drive there to work.

A business park on the edge of a city. ⏻

Out-of-town business parks reduce congestion in city centers, but they increase the amount of traffic on roads because more people use cars to get to work. This causes congestion and pollution (see page 13).

Inner-City Redevelopment

In many inner-city areas, where businesses have moved out, jobs have disappeared and areas have become poorer. Some are now being improved. Old buildings are being pulled down or improved, and new ones built. Inner cities are becoming more attractive places in which to live and work.

A CITY WILDLIFE PARK

Camley Street Natural Park is in the center of London, the UK's capital city. It is a nature reserve, with a pond, meadows, and woods. These provide a habitat for wild plants and animals, such as frogs, butterflies, and bees.

The park was once used to store coal. Then it was a garbage dump. Now it is a protected area where children can study wildlife in the middle of a city.

◑ Camley Street Natural Park is near Kings Cross railroad station in London, UK.

A photographer takes a photo of wildlife in the park. ⊃

Working in Different Places

Some businesses are moving out of city centers to the countryside or smaller towns. This cuts down traffic in cities.

Advances in technology allow others to stop traveling to work in city centers. People who use computers may be able to work from home. They can stay in touch with the office using the Internet and video conferencing (talking over the Internet). This reduces the amount of traveling people do and helps to reduce traffic congestion and pollution.

⊙ **This man is working from home using a laptop computer.**

Activity

FUTURE PLANNING

1. Think about where people live, work, and play in your settlement today.

2. Now imagine it ten years from now. Make a list of how you think it will change.

3. Which changes do you think are good for the environment and which are bad?

The Future

Since towns and cities are constantly growing, we have to keep looking for better ways to protect our environment. If not, we will exhaust the earth's natural resources of food, energy, and water, and pollute the environment with traffic fumes and waste.

We should be careful about how much energy and water we use every day. We should try to produce less waste and recycle more garbage. Our cities need to be carefully planned, and new buildings should be controlled. If this happens, our cities will be attractive places in which to live and work.

An overcrowded street in Tokyo, Japan.

Activity

You can find out how your city, town, or village is protecting the environment and planning for the future. Start by asking your local authority about it. You could ask questions like these:

- How much waste is being recycled?
- Is the local authority going to try to reduce traffic?
- Are there plans to improve the environment?

AN ENVIRONMENTALLY FRIENDLY TOWN

Ecolonia is a small town in the Netherlands, which was built in 1991–92 to use as little energy as possible.

People are allowed to drive cars to their homes, but not through the town center. So most of the streets are just for walkers and cyclists.

The residents have solar panels to heat their water and collect rainwater to use in the home. They recycle almost all of their garbage.

⌂ Houses around the lake in Ecolonia.

Other towns in the Netherlands are copying ideas from Ecolonia to try to become more environmentally friendly.

Glossary

Commercial To do with buying and selling goods and services.

Congestion Too many vehicles or people in a small space.

Country of origin The country where something was grown or made.

Environment Everything in our surroundings.

Environmentally friendly Not damaging to the environment.

Fumes Gas or smoke that is harmful or smells unpleasant.

Greenhouse gases Gases that trap the sun's warmth near the surface of the earth.

Habitat The natural home of a plant or animal.

Import Buy from another country.

Industrial To do with making goods, usually in factories.

Landfill site Garbage dump where solid waste is buried underground.

Nomads People who do not live permanently in one place.

Pollution Damage to air, water, and land by harmful materials.

Recycle To return used materials to be remade and used again.

Rural Belonging to the countryside.

Rush hour Busy times in the mornings and evenings when people travel to and from work.

Solar panels Panels that use energy from the sun's rays to produce electricity. This does not create pollution.

Suburbs Communities next to, or near, a city.

Waste All the material we need to get rid of, such as packaging.

Further Information

Topic Web

MUSIC
- Urban sounds: e.g. car horns, trains, industry
- "Urban" music: e.g. hip-hop, rap, jazz

GEOGRAPHY
- Contrasting different types of settlement
- Land use
- Investigating an issue: out-of-town stores, etc.
- Environmental issues
- How people affect the environment
- Sustainability
- Mapwork

HISTORY
- Development of early settlements
- Growth of towns
- Life in town and country

ARTS & CRAFTS
- View of settlements
- Drawings and models of future cities

DESIGN AND TECHNOLOGY
- House construction
- Design of settlements
- Use of materials

MATH
- Collecting, recording, manipulating, and interpreting data
- Simple statistics

SCIENCE
- Water cycle
- Waste disposal and recycling
- Energy production and use
- Environmental issues: e.g. habitat loss, water pollution, damage to ecosystems, conservation

ENGLISH
- Using settlements as a stimulus for creative writing
- Appropriate poetry
- Library skills

Books

Birth and Death of a City: Settlement Patterns by Elizabeth Raum (Heinemann-Raintree, 2007)

Changing Planet: What Is the Environmental Impact of Human Migration and Settlement? by Sally Morgan (Crabtree Publishing, 2010)

Geography Skills: Looking at Settlements by R. Rees and Judith Anderson (Smart Apple Media, 2007)

Population Patterns: What Factors Determine the Location and Growth of Human Settlements? by Natalie Hyde (Crabtree Publishing, 2010)

Websites

Environmental Education for Kids (EEK!)
http://www.dnr.state.wi.us/org/caer/ce/eek/earth/recycle/waste.htm
Find out all about waste and recycling.

Urbanization
http://youthink.worldbank.org/issues/urbanization
Discover how fast cities are growing across the globe.

Kids and Community
http://www.planning.org/kidsandcommunity/
Learn how cities are planned and created.

Index